CORNERSTONES OF FREEDOM™

STEVE JOBS

BY JOSH GREGORY

CHILDREN'S PRESS®

An Imprint of Scholastic Inc.

New York Toronto London Auckland Sydney
Mexico City New Delhi Hong Kong
Danbury, Connecticut

BRINGING HISTORY to LIFE

Content Consultant
James Marten, PhD
Professor and Chair, History Department
Marquette University
Milwaukee, Wisconsin

Library of Congress Cataloging-in-Publication Data

Gregory, Josh.
  Steve Jobs / by Josh Gregory.
    p. cm.—(Cornerstones of freedom)
  Includes bibliographical references and index.
  ISBN 978-0-531-23606-2 (lib. bdg.) — ISBN 978-0-531-21964-5 (pbk.)
1. Jobs, Steve, 1955–2011—Juvenile literature. 2. Apple Computer,
Inc.—Juvenile literature. 3. Businessmen—United States—Biography—
Juvenile literature. 4. Computer engineers—United States—Biography—
Juvenile literature. 5. Inventors—United States—Biography—Juvenile
literature. I. Title. II. Series: Cornerstones of freedom.
  HD9696.2.U62J63556 2013
  338.7′61004092—dc23[B]   2012034346

Photographs © 2013: Alamy Images: 11 (aerialarchives.com), 49 (david
pearson), 42 (Richard Lewisohn), 5 bottom, 24 (ZUMA Press, Inc.); AP
Images: 34, 57 top (Chris Pizzello), back cover (Evens Lee/Color China
Photo), 18 (Heinz Nixdorf Museumsforum), 10 (Hewlett Packard), 45
(Julie Jacobson), 54 (Mark Lennihan/dapd), 48 (Paul Sakuma), 55 (Rex
Features), 17; Courtesy of Computer History Museum: 16; Corbis Images:
20 (Bettmann), 47 (Chris Hardy/San Francisco Chronicle), 32 (Ed Kashi), 35
(Louie Psihoyos), 29 (Roger Ressmeyer); Getty Images: 15, 56 (Bloomberg),
cover (Christof Stache/AFP), 36 (Diana Walker/SJ/Contour), 43, 57 bottom
(Duffy-Marie Arnoult/WireImage), 40 (John G. Mabanglo/AFP), 2, 3, 7, 26,
50 (Justin Sullivan), 39 (Shahn Kermani), 30 (Ted Thai/Time & Life Pictures),
4 bottom, 14 (Tom Munnecke), 22 (Tony Avelar/Bloomberg); Polaris
Images/Jessica Brandi: 5 top, 8, 13; Superstock, Inc./Tips Images: 6, 51;
The Image Works: 4 top, 25 (Bob Daemmrich), 38 (TopFoto).

Maps by XNR Productions, Inc.

Did you know that studying history can be fun?

BRING HISTORY TO LIFE by becoming a history investigator. Examine the evidence (primary and secondary source materials); cross-examine the people and witnesses. Take a look at what was happening at the time—but be careful! What happened years ago might suddenly become incredibly interesting and change the way you think!

Contents

World Without Computers

Tablet computers, smartphones, and other devices have all become a part of daily life.

Chances are good that you have used a computer sometime today. Maybe you opened your laptop and went online to check your e-mail. Or maybe you downloaded a new song by your favorite band and listened to it on a portable music player. Perhaps you saw something funny on your way to school and used your smartphone to take a picture and send it to a friend. All of these are now common, everyday activities. However, it wasn't all that long ago that they were impossible.

In the early 1970s, the computer technology that makes these activities possible had yet to be invented. In addition, the computers that did exist were far from user-friendly. They took up a huge amount of space and required a great deal of training to use. Many computers even lacked features such as keyboards and screens. Over the next several decades, a group of brilliant young people would push computer technology to incredible new heights. Among them was a forward-thinking man with dreams of changing the world. His name was Steve Jobs.

Steve Jobs played a major role in creating many of the devices we rely on today.

RICHEST COMPANY IN THE WORLD.

CHAPTER 1

GROWING UP

Jobs did not always get good grades in high school, but he had plenty of big ideas.

STEVEN PAUL JOBS WAS BORN on February 24, 1955. His biological parents had decided during the pregnancy to put him up for adoption. Paul and Clara Jobs, a young couple who were unable to have children of their own, adopted Steve upon his birth. They took him home to their apartment in San Francisco, California. Around two years later, they adopted a second child, a girl named Patti. When Steve was about five years old, Paul's employer transferred him to an office in the town of Palo Alto, California. The family packed up and moved to a town nearby.

William Hewlett (left) and David Packard (right) founded Hewlett-Packard, one of the first major companies based in Silicon Valley, California.

The Silicon Valley

During the 1950s, the area south of San Francisco, including Palo Alto and other nearby towns, became home to several growing electronic technology companies. Stanford University, which has made significant contributions to the development of many electronic inventions, is also located in the area. The presence of the tech companies and the university led to the area's nickname, Silicon Valley, after the material used in many electronic devices. In Silicon Valley, Steve Jobs grew up surrounded by electronics. Many of his neighbors worked as **engineers** for major tech companies such as Hewlett-Packard (HP). Others were inventors or hobbyists who tinkered with electronic devices in their garages for fun.

As he grew up, Jobs was fascinated with seeing how things work. He watched carefully as his father rebuilt broken-down cars and made repairs around the house. Paul Jobs taught his son the importance of paying attention to even the smallest details when repairing or building something. He believed that even unseen parts of things, such as a car's engine or a sink's plumbing, should be understandable and function perfectly. Steve learned about cutting-edge electronics from his neighbors, who were sometimes willing to show him

Today, Apple is among the many companies headquartered in Silicon Valley.

the devices they were working on in their garages. As he grew older, Steve began buying do-it-yourself electronics kits and learning how different household items, such as radios and TVs, worked.

Around the time Jobs began high school, a neighbor who worked at HP noticed that Jobs had a real knack for technology. He introduced Jobs to an HP-sponsored group called the Explorers Club. The Explorers Club was a small group of students who, like Jobs, were interested in technology. At meetings, the students listened to HP engineers discuss new inventions and they shared ideas about their own tech projects. It was here that Jobs saw a desktop computer for the first time. It was nothing like the powerful machines we use today, though. In fact, Jobs later described it as "a glorified calculator."

First Steps

With the encouragement of the people who ran the Explorers Club, Jobs started working on an electronic device of his own. However, he had trouble finding all of the parts he needed to complete the project. He decided that the best way to get the parts was to go straight to the source. He opened up a local phone book and found the number for Bill Hewlett, the chief executive officer (CEO) of HP. Though Hewlett was a busy, highly successful business leader, he listened to Jobs's request and agreed to get him the parts he needed. Hewlett was so impressed with the young inventor that he also offered Jobs a summer job at HP. Each day during the

Jobs began learning valuable business skills as a high school student.

summer between his freshman and sophomore years of high school, Jobs worked on an assembly line at the HP factory. There, he got a firsthand look at how electronic devices were produced on a large scale.

After beginning his sophomore year of high school, Jobs began working at a local electronics store. There, he quickly learned the values of different electronic parts, or components. He often haggled over prices with customers at the store. He became so good at spotting the value of different pieces that he could buy electronic devices cheaply at local flea markets, harvest the valuable parts, and resell them to his boss at the store for a profit. These business instincts would serve him well in his later endeavors.

The Perfect Partner

Not surprisingly, Jobs chose to enroll in an electronics class in high school the first chance he got. He often rebelled against the teacher, and he wasn't a very good student. However, taking the class would turn out to be one of the best decisions Jobs ever made. Through one of the other students in the class, Jobs was introduced to a computer expert named Steve Wozniak. Wozniak was five years older than Jobs and had a much deeper understanding of electronics. He had attended the same high school and taken the same computer class that Jobs was enrolled in. Unlike Jobs, however, Wozniak was one of the teacher's favorite students. While Jobs was rebellious and enjoyed arguing with people, Wozniak was shy and calm.

Jobs developed a lasting friendship with Steve Wozniak (right) based on a shared love of electronics, practical jokes, and rock music.

Despite the differences in their personalities, the two Steves quickly became friends. They both had a strong interest in electronics, and they enjoyed listening to the same kinds of music. They also shared a love of playing practical jokes. Before too long, they began teaming up to work on electronics projects in their parents' garages. One of the first devices they built was a box that tricked telephones into making long-distance calls for free. Jobs came up with the idea, while Wozniak handled most of the technical work. At first, they just used it to make prank calls

SPOTLIGHT ON

Steve Wozniak

Steve Wozniak was born in 1950. The son of an engineer, he became interested in electronics at a very young age. As a fifth-grader, he built an electronic intercom system that ran between his and five friends' bedrooms. By the time he was a senior in high school, he had a job at Sylvania, a large electronics company. He quit college after two years and began building computers in his garage. Soon afterward, he met Steve Jobs, beginning a partnership that would bring them both incredible wealth.

Though instrumental to Apple's early success, Wozniak was not interested in running a major company. Beginning in the early 1980s, his role at Apple grew smaller and smaller. Since then, he has kept busy with other businesses and charitable organizations.

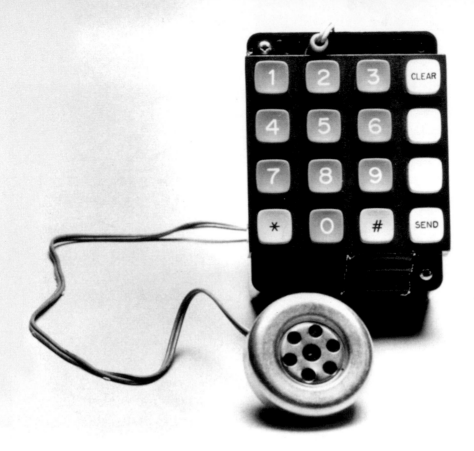

The telephone box was the first project Jobs and Wozniak worked on together that made money.

to people all around the world. But Jobs soon realized that they could make a profit by building and selling the devices. They made 100 boxes at a cost of $40 each and sold them for $150 apiece. Their first project together had proven to be a success.

Off to College . . . and Back Again

Jobs graduated from high school in 1972. At first, he wasn't sure he wanted to attend college. However, his parents convinced him that it was important to get a good education. Jobs enrolled at Reed College in

Portland, Oregon. Soon after classes started, however, he found that he didn't enjoy the experience. He liked to learn, but he hated being forced to take courses he wasn't interested in. He officially dropped out of school but continued going to the classes he enjoyed. In February 1974, he left college for good and returned to his parents' home in Palo Alto.

Not long after his return home, Jobs was hired at Atari, a successful video game company. He didn't get along well with most of his co-workers, but his bosses liked him because he produced good work. After saving up some money, he quit his job and traveled to India, where he lived a simple lifestyle and studied Hinduism. Seven months later, he returned home and

SPOTLIGHT ON

Atari

Founded in 1972, Atari created some of the world's first coin-operated video games and revolutionized home video game **consoles** with the introduction of *Pong*. The home version of *Pong* was a console containing a single built-in game. Its success led to the development of the Atari Video Computer System (VCS), later known as the Atari 2600. The VCS was released in 1978. Unlike the *Pong* machine, it contained a cartridge slot that allowed users to plug in a variety of games, which could be purchased separately. Atari continued to be a leader in the video game industry until the early 1980s, when its dominance was overshadowed by the rise of companies such as Nintendo.

asked for his old job back. Though they were surprised that Jobs wanted to return to his former job, his old bosses were happy to have him back at the company. They asked him to develop a new, single-player version of their most famous two-player game, *Pong*. Jobs knew the perfect person to help him with the project. He called up Steve Wozniak, who agreed to help create the new game. Together, they finished it in less than four days.

Getting Personal

In 1975, a computer called the Altair 8800 was released. It was little more than a box with lights and switches on

The Altair 8800 was popular among computer hobbyists during the early 1970s.

A FIRSTHAND LOOK AT
THE ALTAIR 8800

The Altair 8800 might not seem impressive compared to today's computers, but it was a major inspiration for some of the computer industry's most important inventions. See page 60 for a link to watch the Altair 8800 in action.

the front. It was intended for use by computer hobbyists and businesses, and was of no use to most people. However, Wozniak was amazed by the power and small size of its **microprocessor**. He realized that such a device could be used to create a small computer that would fit on a desk and attach to a monitor and keyboard. He began developing the computer at home in his spare time. By the end of June 1975, Wozniak had completed a working version of his invention.

Jobs was amazed at Wozniak's new computer. He began suggesting small ways to improve it. He also helped out by tracking down hard-to-find computer parts for low prices. Wozniak wanted to share the designs with his fellow computer enthusiasts. He was only building the machine for fun and wanted others to have a chance to work with his new technology. Jobs convinced him to keep the designs a secret. He suggested they form their own computer company and sell the machine, just as they had with their phone device several years earlier. This time, however, Jobs knew they had a much bigger product on their hands.

CHAPTER 2

THE BIRTH OF APPLE

Jobs and Wozniak join Apple president John Sculley (center) in showing off one of their designs at a 1984 conference.

THE TWO STEVES DECIDED TO name their company Apple Computer. Jobs had worked at an apple farm from time to time after graduating high school, and he thought apples would make people think of fun and friendliness rather than difficult-to-use technology.

From the very beginning, Apple was unlike other businesses. Jobs and Wozniak refused to clean up their appearances or change their habits. Both had long, shaggy hair, and Jobs often refused to bathe or wear deodorant. Potential customers weren't sure they could trust these disheveled young men. But thanks to Jobs's incredible ability to persuade people, they eventually convinced a local computer shop to order 50 of their Apple I computers. With this order—and a little money that Jobs and Wozniak raised by selling some of their possessions—the business was officially off and running.

Jobs designed the Apple II's case to look simple and streamlined.

In the Garage

Jobs and Wozniak assembled their computers in the same garage where Jobs had once spent hours watching his father work on cars. Their earliest models did not come with keyboards or monitors. Instead, they were solely circuit boards that people could buy and use to build their own computer systems. Most of the people who bought the Apple I were fellow computer hobbyists who wanted to see what the new machines could do. Word slowly began to spread that Apple computers were something special. Soon, people around the country were watching to see what Jobs and Wozniak would come up with next.

By the fall of 1976, Wozniak had begun working on a new model. The Apple II's most striking advantage over the Apple I was its ability to display color images on a screen. Jobs, meanwhile, was thinking of ways to sell the computers to people who weren't technology geeks. He realized that the average person didn't have the knowledge to assemble a computer system. He thought that if Apple could create a machine that came preassembled in a well-designed case, the company could change the way people thought about computers.

Jobs decided that the case should be made of plastic, rather than the steel usually available from manufacturers. The case should have a visually appealing design that would look nice sitting on a desk. Following the advice he had learned from his father, he insisted that even the unseen interior parts, such as the circuit board, be arranged perfectly. To build such a computer, Apple needed money. Once again putting his powers of persuasion to work, Jobs was able to secure $200,000 from a wealthy investor.

In April 1977, Apple was ready to reveal its new computer to the world. Jobs and Wozniak attended a computer trade show, where many technology companies gathered to show off their latest products. They set up the Apple II at their booth. Behind them hung a display showing their clever new logo: a bright, multicolored apple with a bite taken out of it. The Apple II was a huge hit among the people at the trade show. By the end of the day, Jobs and Wozniak had sold 300 units.

The Apple Logo

Before the release of the Apple II, Apple's logo was very different from the one that is now famous. Instead of today's simple Apple shape, the logo was a detailed drawing of the scientist Isaac Newton sitting beneath an apple tree. A single apple dangled above Newton's head.

Steve Jobs knew that his company would need a more immediately recognizable logo to help people spot its products. During the development of the Apple II, he hired a public relations company to help define Apple's image. One of the company's art directors designed a colorful version of the same logo that Apple continues to use today.

A Real Company

Businesses and families alike were impressed by the power and simplicity of the Apple II. The company was soon making enough money to move out of the Jobs family's garage and into a real office. The two Steves were also able to hire some employees to help them. Because neither Jobs nor Wozniak had ever run a large business before, they hired an experienced businessperson to serve as president of the company. By the end of the year, Apple had sold more than 2,500 Apple II computers. Over the next 16 years, the company would sell more than 16 million.

Just as Apple was taking off, Jobs's first child was born. For many years, he played a limited role in raising his daughter Lisa.

In the meantime, Apple's success skyrocketed. Consistently strong Apple II sales allowed the company to expand further and further. Jobs and Wozniak became millionaires. By the late 1970s, Apple had three new projects in development. One of them was a small, inexpensive computer called the Macintosh, or the Mac.

In 1979, an electronics technology company named Xerox became an investor in Apple. As a result, some of

Apple II computers were especially popular in schools.

The original Xerox mouse was much boxier and less comfortable to use than today's mice.

Apple's top employees, including Jobs, got a chance to see some of the projects that Xerox was working on. The most impressive thing they saw was a computer with a graphical user **interface** (GUI). Until then, computers were controlled entirely with text commands. Users typed words and symbols into the computer to instruct it what to do. But with Xerox's invention, users could operate a device called a mouse to point and click on graphical objects shown on the computer screen.

Back at Apple, engineers immediately began working to incorporate GUIs and mice into their projects. Jobs was especially excited about the new technology. He realized that it would make computers easier to use than ever before. Instead of memorizing text commands, people could manage computer files by clicking on familiar objects such as folders and trash cans. Users would automatically understand what these **icons** were

A VIEW FROM ABR☆AD

While working on the Macintosh, Steve Jobs took a trip to Japan with other Apple engineers to visit several electronics companies. They hoped to find a company that could manufacture disk drives for the Macintosh.

The difficult aspects of Jobs's personality came out in full force during the trip. He refused to wear a suit to meetings and sometimes even insulted a product in front of the company that made it. Most of the businesspeople Jobs met on that trip were upset by his behavior. Like many others, they eventually came to realize that this was typical behavior from Jobs.

for because they looked like objects from the real world. Over the next couple of years, Jobs and his team worked to create the perfect GUI for the Mac's **operating system**.

Ready to Launch

In November 1983, the **software** company Microsoft announced that it was working on a new operating system called Windows. Its GUI looked very similar to the one Apple was designing for the Mac. Jobs was furious. He accused Microsoft founder Bill Gates of stealing his ideas. From then on, the two companies were major rivals in the computer industry.

About two months later, the Macintosh was finally ready to be released. Just as Jobs predicted, people were amazed by how easy the computer was to use and how many useful things it could do. The launch was a huge success, and the Mac sold extremely well over the next few months.

Hard to Handle

Riding high on his success, Jobs began involving himself in more areas of Apple's business. Many Apple employees became irritated with him. Jobs had a very forceful personality, and he was quick to anger. It was not uncommon for

A FIRSTHAND LOOK AT THE MACINTOSH SUPER BOWL COMMERCIAL

Directed by filmmaker Ridley Scott, the Macintosh commercial that aired during the 1984 Super Bowl introduced the world to a computer unlike any that had come before. See page 60 for a link to watch the commercial online.

The original Macintosh model was very successful at first.

him to scream at his employees and insult them harshly if he was even a little unhappy with their work. He also had a habit of taking credit for ideas that other people came up with. To make matters worse, Mac sales began to slow down as 1984 wound to a close. Many of the computers were overheating, causing them to stop working. Apple's president and board of directors placed some of the blame on Jobs. Just months after one of his greatest successes, Jobs was headed for one of his biggest disappointments.

CHAPTER 3
MOVING ON

Leaving Apple behind was a hard decision for Jobs to make.

BECAUSE JOBS WAS UNABLE to get along with many of the employees, the leaders of Apple tried to convince him to take over a new division of the company. That division would focus on coming up with new ideas. This would keep him out of the company's day-to-day business while still making use of his considerable talent. Jobs rejected the idea. After he failed in an attempt to take control of the company himself, the board of directors took away almost all of his responsibilities. While he was still technically employed at Apple, he was unable to have any effect on the company. Jobs decided he would rather quit than be put in a position where he couldn't accomplish anything. On September 13, 1985, he resigned from the company he had co-founded less than a decade earlier.

Jobs hired trusted Apple employees to form his NeXT team.

A New Idea

While working on the Mac, Jobs had gotten to know several college professors who led advanced research projects. They told him that they would be able to perform experiments more efficiently if they had access to powerful computers. Instead of taking time to actually perform certain experiments, the scientists could use the computers to simulate them. This would produce the same results without taking up as much time or as many resources. However, the only computers powerful enough to simulate experiments were far too expensive for most universities to afford.

After leaving Apple, Jobs decided to start a new company that would design computers to fill this need in the educational market. He convinced several Apple employees who had helped work on the Mac to quit their jobs and join his new company, which he named NeXT.

Jobs envisioned the NeXT computer as a black cube. It would come with a variety of programs useful to professors and students. It would also have its own operating system for which software companies could easily make programs.

Two Companies

In the fall of 1985, around the same time he was working to get NeXT off the ground, Jobs took a tour of the computer graphics division of Lucasfilm. This company was owned by *Star Wars* creator George Lucas. Lucas was hoping to sell the division, and Jobs was impressed with what he saw. The employees of this division developed software and **hardware** for creating advanced computer graphics. Some of the team members, including a former Disney animator named John Lasseter, also used the technology to create their own animated short films.

During the negotiations, Lucas warned Jobs that the team seemed to show more interest in creating the short films than it did in developing new technology. The warning failed to frighten Jobs away. He spent $10 million to purchase and fund the Lucasfilm computer division, which was renamed Pixar. With both Pixar and NeXT, Jobs was running two companies at the same time.

John Lasseter

John Lasseter was first drawn to animation as a high school student, when he read a book about Disney's 1959 film *Sleeping Beauty*. Fittingly, he would begin his animation career working for Disney. Between 1979 and 1983, he worked on traditionally animated Disney films. In 1984, he took a job in Lucasfilm's computer graphics division, which eventually became Pixar. In addition to his early short films, Lasseter also directed Pixar movie hits such as *Toy Story*, *A Bug's Life*, and *Cars*. In 2006, Disney purchased Pixar, bringing Lasseter back to the company that had kicked off his career.

At first, Pixar's main business was centered on creating computer graphics hardware. The company sold its products to animators, graphic designers, and even medical companies, which used the computers to create informational displays on medical equipment.

In 1986, Jobs asked Lasseter to develop a short film that would show off Pixar's technology. Jobs hoped that the film would help Pixar sell more hardware, but it would soon prove to be more successful than he could have imagined.

Lasseter's film was called *Luxo Jr.* Just over two minutes long, it tells the story of a small desk lamp that plays with a ball as the lamp's father watches. As Jobs had hoped, it showed off the power of Pixar's technology. However, it was also a major critical success.

A FIRSTHAND LOOK AT
PIXAR'S SHORT FILMS

Even after its success with feature-length films, Pixar has continued to make new short films at a steady rate. See page 60 for a link to watch clips from these films online.

A few months after its release, *Luxo Jr.* became the first computer-generated film to be nominated for an Academy Award, though it did not win.

Jobs loved the film just as much as the critics had. He encouraged Lasseter to continue working on new projects. In 1987, Pixar's short film *Red's Dream* was released. It followed the tale of a red unicycle that dreams of life in the circus. In 1988, Pixar released

Jobs realized that Pixar had the potential to do much more than just design computer graphics systems.

Lasseter's third short film, *Tin Toy*. This story of a mechanical toy won the company its first Academy Award. Jobs began to realize that Pixar's future lay not in creating computer technology, but in making films.

Starting a Family

In 1989, while giving a lecture at the Stanford University business school, Jobs met a woman named Laurene Powell. He was immediately interested in her, and the two went on a date after the lecture. Around two years later, on March 18, 1991, they were married. A few months later, Laurene gave birth to a baby boy named Reed. Having improved his relationship with his daughter, Lisa, Jobs invited her to come live with the family the following year.

Jobs and Laurene Powell shared a long marriage.

At the Movies

The NeXT computer was finally ready to release in mid-1989. However, a high price and a lack of available software made it a major flop. By the following year, the company was losing money at an alarming rate. Jobs decided to stop manufacturing the computers. NeXT was out of the hardware business, but it remained active by **licensing** its powerful operating system to the computer company IBM.

Though NeXT had not met his expectations, Jobs knew that he still had a chance for major success with Pixar. In 1991, Disney agreed to help fund a full-length feature film from the Pixar team. Lasseter had an idea to make a movie about a group of toys that could move and talk when people weren't around. It would be called *Toy Story*.

After several years of hard work, *Toy Story* premiered in 1995. It was an instant success. Critics and audiences alike were amazed by the incredible computer animation and were drawn in by the movie's story and characters. It had a higher box office **gross** than any other movie released that year.

That same year marked another milestone in Jobs's life. He and his wife welcomed a new baby daughter named Erin into their family.

Familiar Faces

While Jobs had found great success by the mid-1990s, the company he had helped start was not so lucky. In the years since Jobs had resigned, Apple had fallen far

YESTERDAY'S HEADLINES

Upon its release, *Toy Story* was met with praise from almost every film critic who reviewed it. These critics wrote glowingly of the film's remarkable animation style while also admiring its memorable characters and thrilling story. Roger Ebert gave the film four stars, his highest rating. He wrote that he "felt [he] was in at the dawn of a new era of movie animation, which draws on the best of cartoons and reality, creating a world somewhere in between, where space not only bends but snaps, crackles and pops."

from its position as the world's top personal computer company. Microsoft and its Windows operating system had come to dominate the market.

In 1996, Apple was working on a new computer that it hoped would mark a change of fortune. However, it needed a new operating system to pair with its new hardware. Rather than create a new system from scratch, Apple's leaders decided to purchase the work of another company. Among the several operating systems they examined was the one created by NeXT. After a round of negotiations, Apple offered to purchase the entire company to gain its operating system and its skilled employees. As part of the deal, Jobs returned to Apple as an adviser.

Many of the former NeXT employees were given important positions at Apple. Within a few months, Apple decided to fire its CEO, who had been doing a poor job of leading the company. The board of directors offered the CEO position to Jobs. At first, he refused the offer. Then, in September 1997, he agreed to serve as CEO until the company could find a suitable replacement. Almost exactly 12 years after leaving, Steve Jobs was once again ready to lead Apple into the future.

NeXT provided Jobs with a path back to leadership at Apple.

CHAPTER 4

BACK AT APPLE

The first iMac was one of Jobs's first projects after returning to Apple.

THE FIRST THING JOBS DID

upon returning to Apple was simplify the company's line of products. At the time, Apple sold a wide variety of different computers. Each had a different model name. Jobs believed that was confusing to consumers. He determined that the company should offer just four computers: two laptops and two desktop machines.

Jony Ive (right) and Jobs shared many of the same ideas about product design.

He also took an immediate liking to an Apple designer named Jonathan "Jony" Ive. Ive shared Jobs's love of simple, elegant machines that both looked nice and functioned well. They worked together to create a new desktop computer called the iMac. Like the original Macintosh, it was a full computer system built into a single case. When it was released in August 1998, it was an immediate success. Apple was back on its way to the top.

Big Plans

The year 1998 also saw the birth of Jobs's fourth child, a daughter named Eve. It took a lot of effort for Jobs to balance his family life with his responsibilities at Apple and Pixar, but he did his best to make the situation work. Even when putting in very long hours on the job, he made sure to set time aside for his family.

In late 1999, Jobs began planning Apple's next big move. He decided that the best way to showcase the company's unique products was to open a series of **retail** stores that sold only Apple devices. Jobs wanted to build the stores in shopping malls and along busy streets to attract lots of window shoppers. He believed that once they saw Apple computers in action, shoppers would immediately want to purchase the devices for themselves. Jobs also wanted to make sure that each store was designed to fit Apple's image.

Jony Ive

Jonathan "Jony" Ive grew up in a small town near London, England. Even as a child, he dreamed of one day becoming a designer. After using a Mac for the first time while attending college, he felt an immediate connection to Apple's design.

Ive began working at Apple in 1992 and quickly worked his way up through the design department. When Steve Jobs returned to the company in 1997, the two formed a close bond almost immediately. Ive and Jobs worked together closely to come up with many new product designs, from the see-through case of the first iMac to the aluminum and glass form of the iPad. Today, Ive remains one of Apple's top employees, serving as the head of the company's design department.

In January 2000, Apple revealed its newest operating system, called OS X. Built using many of the features of NeXT's operating system, it would become the backbone of all Apple computers. That same year, Jobs began another major project. Noticing that more and more people were using computers to copy CDs and play music, he led the development of a new program called iTunes. iTunes could be used to copy music files from CDs, and then either to play the files directly from the computer or burn them to blank CDs. While other programs with these features already existed, they were sometimes difficult to use and lacked Apple's sleek design. When iTunes was released in January 2001, Mac users instantly took a liking to its simple interface. With Apple's first venture into the music business proving to be a success, Jobs began planning for a much bigger leap forward.

New Products and a Place to Buy Them

On May 19, 2001, the first Apple retail store opened in Tysons Corner Center in Virginia. Unlike most computer stores of the time, it was a bright, welcoming space that allowed shoppers to get a hands-on look at Apple's products. The stores were organized into sections based on different things people could do with Apple computers, such as listen to music or edit video footage. The stores were an immediate hit with shoppers, and Apple's sales continued to increase.

Around five months later, Jobs showed off his latest creation: a portable music player that could hold around 1,000 songs. While similar music players had been on the market for several years, most models were either large and bulky or they didn't hold many songs. The

The iPod changed the way that many people listen to music.

iPod, on the other hand, was small and still held plenty of music. It was a success, and within a few years it would become Apple's biggest moneymaker.

As the iPod grew in popularity, Jobs recognized another way for Apple to take advantage of changes in the music industry. At the time, most people downloaded music illegally from untrustworthy sources. Illegal music files often had poor sound quality and could be difficult to obtain. But there were few legal options for downloading music files. Jobs believed that if people were offered an easy way to download files legally, they would be willing to pay for the music they loaded onto their iPods. He knew that such a service would need to offer high sound quality and include features such as cover artwork. Jobs thought that customers should also be allowed to purchase individual songs instead of only whole albums. Most importantly, the service would need the support of all of the major record labels, which controlled the production and legal distribution of music.

At first, the labels were reluctant to go along with Apple's plan. They didn't want to give Apple a portion of the money they received from selling music, and they didn't like Jobs's plan to sell single songs for $0.99 each. However, the record company executives were no match for Jobs. He used his persuasive personality to convince all five of the world's biggest record labels to put their music up for sale on Apple's iTunes Store.

The store went online on April 28, 2003. Within a week, more than a million songs had been sold. Once again, Jobs's instincts had proven correct, and the way people buy music was changed forever.

Bad News

Since returning to Apple, Jobs had overseen one successful project after another. But in October 2003, everything changed for him when he was diagnosed with **pancreatic** cancer. At first, doctors believed that it would be easy to treat with surgery, because they had discovered it at a fairly early stage. But Jobs stubbornly refused

Jobs introduced the iTunes Music Store at a 2003 presentation.

to undergo surgery to remove the cancer. Instead, he attempted to fight the illness by eating healthy foods and taking a variety of natural medicines. These methods did not help, however, and the cancer only worsened.

In July 2004, Jobs finally allowed doctors to operate to remove the cancer from his body. When the surgeons cut him open, they discovered that the cancer had spread to other parts of his body, including his liver. They removed what they could, but they could not cure him completely. Jobs decided to keep his illness a secret from the public. He told everyone, except his family and a few trusted friends, that he had made a full recovery.

Touch Screens and Talking

Refusing to let his illness keep him down, Jobs went back to work immediately after recovering from surgery. Seeing that certain new cell phones were equipped with built-in music players, he grew concerned that the iPod would soon become **obsolete**. He asked Apple engineers to begin working on a cellular phone modeled after the iPod. It would be called the iPhone.

The iPhone combined the features of an iPod and a cell phone.

Since its introduction, the iPhone has become Apple's most successful product.

At first, the engineers tried to use the iPod's wheel-shaped button arrangement on the new phone. But they had trouble finding a way to use these controls to dial phone numbers or type text messages. At the same time, another group of engineers was hard at work on a touch screen device that users could control by making different movements with their fingers. Jobs eventually realized that this touch screen technology was perfect for the iPhone. Despite a high price tag, the iPhone was yet another huge success for Apple when it was released in June 2007.

As Apple grew more and more successful, Jobs's health continued to worsen. He began losing weight, making it obvious to people who saw him that

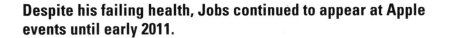

Despite his failing health, Jobs continued to appear at Apple events until early 2011.

something was wrong. However, he still refused to explain his illness to anyone outside his close circle of friends and family. In March 2009, he had a liver transplant. The operation improved his health, but he was still far from cured.

In January 2010, Jobs unveiled a new Apple product known as the iPad. It used the same operating system as the iPhone, but had a much larger screen and could not make phone calls. The large screen allowed people to read books and magazines, watch videos, surf the Internet, and perform many other activities. The new device was yet another success in Jobs's long string of popular inventions, selling around 15 million units in the first nine months.

Over the next few months, Jobs's health went into rapid decline. By the end of 2010, he weighed just 115 pounds, and doctors continued to find more and more cancer in his body. He tried to work anyway, but he was finally forced to leave his beloved company in early 2011. Though he continued to undergo treatments, the cancer could not be beaten. After a long struggle, Jobs died on October 5, 2011, at the age of 56. People around the globe mourned the loss of a man whose inventions had changed the world.

TODAY'S PERSPECTIVE

When the iPad was first unveiled to the public, many people were skeptical of the device. Bloggers with sites devoted to electronic technology wrote posts wondering what the point of it was and why it lacked certain features. Many writers questioned how the iPad would be different from an iPhone. Some even predicted that it would be Apple's first big flop in years.

Jobs was upset by the reaction to the device, but he did not need to worry. Consumers instantly understood the appeal of the device when they used it. Once the iPad went on sale, it became a huge hit.

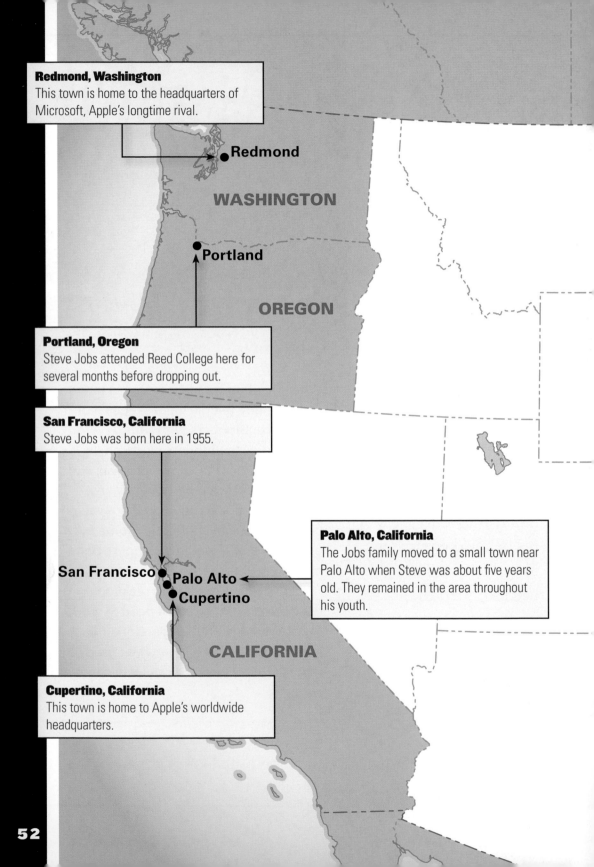

Redmond, Washington
This town is home to the headquarters of Microsoft, Apple's longtime rival.

● Redmond

WASHINGTON

● Portland

OREGON

Portland, Oregon
Steve Jobs attended Reed College here for several months before dropping out.

San Francisco, California
Steve Jobs was born here in 1955.

Palo Alto, California
The Jobs family moved to a small town near Palo Alto when Steve was about five years old. They remained in the area throughout his youth.

San Francisco ● Palo Alto ← ● Cupertino

CALIFORNIA

Cupertino, California
This town is home to Apple's worldwide headquarters.

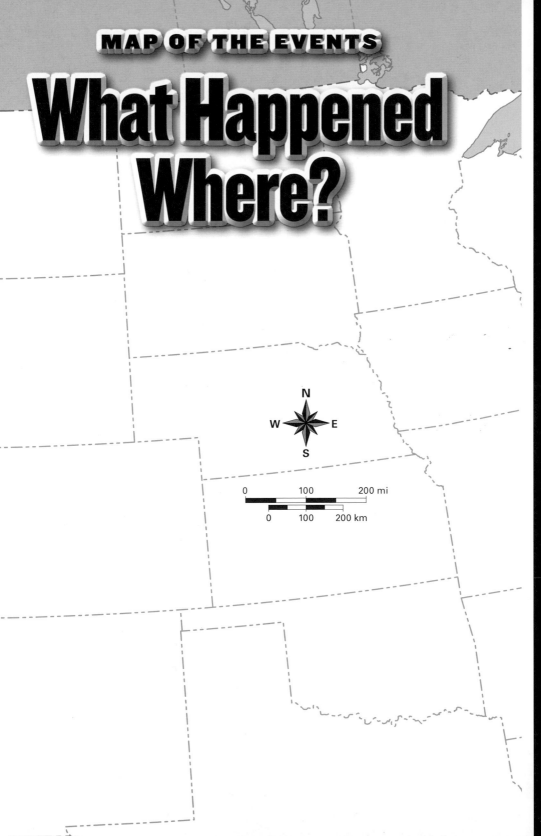

What Happened Where?

N
W   E
S

0   100   200 mi

0   100   200 km

Then and Now

Tim Cook has served as CEO of Apple since Jobs left the company.

Even after Jobs's death, Apple has continued to be a major innovator in the world of technology. Jobs was replaced as CEO by Tim Cook, who had been a crucial Apple employee for many years. Other close associates of Jobs, such as Jony Ive, continue to steer the company in the direction that Jobs outlined during his leadership.

TIM COOK HAS ALSO WORKED FOR

The influence of Steve Jobs can be seen in a variety of industries, from computers to cell phones to music. As a young man, Jobs dreamed of changing the world. With hard work and a unique way of looking at the world, he was able to achieve this goal several times over. Thanks to his efforts, the way people use technology in their everyday lives will never be the same.

Jobs's fans paid tribute to his life by leaving apples outside Apple stores around the world.

You will be missed Steve
-Austin, USA

INFLUENTIAL INDIVIDUALS

Steve Wozniak

Bill Hewlett (1913–2001) was one of the founders of Hewlett-Packard. When Steve Jobs was a teenager, Hewlett offered him a summer job working at HP after being impressed by his ambition and work ethic.

Paul Jobs (1931–) was Steve Jobs's father. His lessons in rebuilding cars and doing household repairs were a major influence on his son's design sensibilities.

Steve Wozniak (1950–) is a co-founder of Apple. His work on the Apple I and Apple II computers helped establish the company as a major force in the computer industry.

Bill Gates (1955–) is the co-founder of Microsoft who, along with Steve Jobs and others, helped to revolutionize the world of personal computers.

John Lasseter (1957–) is an animator whose films helped establish Pixar as a major force in the entertainment industry. He currently oversees both Pixar and Walt Disney Animation Studios.

Laurene Powell Jobs (1963–) was the wife of Steve Jobs and is the mother of three of his four children. She is also involved in several nonprofit organizations.

John Lasseter

Jony Ive (1967–) is a designer who worked closely with Steve Jobs in the 1990s and 2000s to create almost all of Apple's signature devices. He remains one of the company's most influential employees.

Jony Ive

TIMELINE

1955

February 24
Steve Jobs is born in San Francisco, California.

1975

June 29
Steve Wozniak completes the first working prototype for the Apple I computer.

1977

April
The Apple II computer is unveiled at a trade show.

1985

Jobs resigns from Apple; in the fall, Jobs purchases Pixar.

1989

The NeXT computer is released.

1991

Jobs marries Laurene Powell; their son, Reed, is born a few months later.

2000

January
The OS X operating system is unveiled.

2001

iTunes is released; the first Apple retail store opens; the iPod is unveiled.

2003

The iTunes store goes online; Jobs is diagnosed with pancreatic cancer in October.

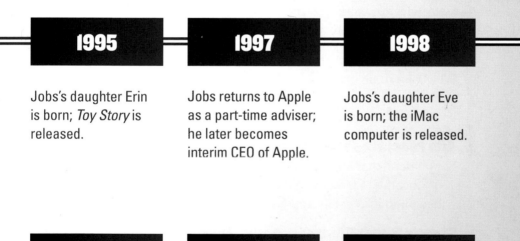

1978

May 17
Jobs's first daughter, Lisa Brennan, is born.

1984

A Macintosh television commercial premieres during the Super Bowl game; two days later, the Macintosh computer is released.

1995

Jobs's daughter Erin is born; *Toy Story* is released.

1997

Jobs returns to Apple as a part-time adviser; he later becomes interim CEO of Apple.

1998

Jobs's daughter Eve is born; the iMac computer is released.

2007

January
The iPhone is unveiled.

2010

January
The iPad is unveiled.

2011

October 5
Jobs dies of cancer.

LIVING HISTORY

Primary sources provide firsthand evidence about a topic.
Witnesses to a historical event create primary sources. They include
autobiographies, newspaper reports of the time, oral histories,
photographs, and memoirs. A secondary source analyzes primary
sources, and is one step or more removed from the event. Secondary
sources include textbooks, encyclopedias, and commentaries.
To view the following primary and secondary sources, go to
www.factsfornow.scholastic.com. Enter the keywords **Steve Jobs** and
look for the Living History logo ∑¡.

∑¡ The Altair 8800 The Altair 8800 computer was one of Steve
Wozniak's main inspirations for designing the original Apple I
computer. You can watch a video and listen to sound clips of this
early computer in action.

∑¡ The Macintosh Super Bowl Commercial The Macintosh
commercial that aired during the Super Bowl in January
1984 became legendary in the advertising world and created
widespread interest in Apple's personal computers.

∑¡ Pixar's Short Films Pixar's early short films helped the
company gain recognition for its exceptional animation. Pixar
continues to make short films today, and many samples are
available for viewing online.

∑¡ Steve Jobs's 2005 Stanford Commencement Speech
In 2005, Steve Jobs spoke to the graduating class at Stanford
University. He took the opportunity to discuss some of the most
important moments in his life.

RESOURCES

Books

Lakin, Patricia. *Steve Jobs: Thinking Differently*. New York: Aladdin, 2012.

Pollack, Pam and Meg Belviso. *Who Was Steve Jobs?* New York: Grosset & Dunlap, 2012.

Venezia, Mike. *Steve Jobs & Steve Wozniak: Geek Heroes Who Put the Personal in Computers*. New York: Children's Press, 2010.

Ziller, Amanda. *Steve Jobs: American Genius*. New York: Collins, 2012.

Visit this Scholastic Web site for more information on Steve Jobs: www.factsfornow.scholastic.com Enter the keywords Steve Jobs

GLOSSARY

consoles (KAHN-sohlz) cabinets for something electronic, such as a television or computer, designed to stand on the floor

engineers (en-juh-NEERZ) people who are trained to design and build things

gross (GROHS) total amount of money earned

hardware (HAHRD-wair) computer equipment

icons (EYE-kahnz) graphic symbols representing programs, functions, or files on a computer

interface (IN-tur-fase) a way of interacting with a computer system

licensing (LYE-suhn-sing) allowing other companies to make use of a property in exchange for money

microprocessor (mye-kroh-PRAH-ses-ur) a computer chip that controls the functions of an electronic device

obsolete (ahb-suh-LEET) out-of-date; no longer made or used because something new has been invented

operating system (AH-puh-ray-ting SIS-tuhm) a master control program on a computer that allows other programs to run on the computer

pancreatic (pan-kree-AT-ik) having to do with the pancreas, a digestive gland located near the stomach

retail (REE-tayl) having to do with the sale of goods directly to customers

software (SAWFT-wair) computer programs

INDEX

Page numbers in *italics* indicate illustrations.

ABOUT THE AUTHOR

Josh Gregory writes and edits books for kids.
He lives in Chicago, Illinois.